From Your Friends at *The Mailbox*®
Vocabulary & Spelling MIND BUILDERS
Grades 4–6

Welcome to *Vocabulary and Spelling Mind Builders*! This must-have resource is sure to reinforce vocabulary and spelling skills while developing critical-thinking skills. Packed with curriculum-based problems and puzzles covering a variety of vocabulary and spelling topics, this resource provides students with a school year's worth of mind-building opportunities.

Project Manager:
Peggy W. Hambright

Writer:
Ann Fisher

Art Coordinator:
Pam Crane

Artists:
Teresa R. Davidson, Nolan Galloway, Barry Slate

Cover Artists:
Nick Greenwood, Clevell Harris, Kimberly Richard

www.themailbox.com

©2001 by THE EDUCATION CENTER, INC.
All rights reserved.
ISBN #1-56234-438-2

Except as provided for herein, no part of this publication may be reproduced or transmitted in any form or by any means, electronic or mechanical, including photocopying, recording, or storing in any information storage and retrieval system or electronic online bulletin board, without prior written permission from The Education Center, Inc. Permission is given to the original purchaser to reproduce patterns and reproducibles for individual classroom use only and not for resale or distribution. Reproduction for an entire school or school system is prohibited. Please direct written inquiries to The Education Center, Inc., P.O. Box 9753, Greensboro, NC 27429-0753. The Education Center®, *The Mailbox*®, and the mailbox/post/grass logo are registered trademarks of The Education Center, Inc. All other brand or product names are trademarks or registered trademarks of their respective companies.

Manufactured in the United States

TABLE OF CONTENTS

Context Clues	3–9
Synonyms & Antonyms	10–16
Homophones	17–23
Prefixes & Suffixes	24–30
Word Origins	31–37
Figures of Speech	38–43
Answer Keys	44–48

HOW TO USE THIS BOOK

Inside you will find an assortment of problems designed to reinforce the vocabulary and spelling topics and skills that you teach. Each activity page features five mind-building vocabulary and spelling problems plus a more difficult bonus builder problem to boost students' critical-thinking skills.

Use the activity pages in this book in a variety of ways to supplement your vocabulary and spelling curriculum.

For independent practice, duplicate the activity pages for students to use as morning work, problems of the day, free-time activities, or daily homework practice.

For partner or small-group practice, duplicate a desired activity page and give each pair or group a copy. Have students discuss possible answers for the problems.

For whole-group practice, make transparencies of the activity pages.

For a learning center activity, duplicate, laminate, and cut apart the activity pages. Group the resulting cards by topic and place specific skill cards at a center. Or, for a mixed review, place a variety of skill cards at a center.

For assessing students' understanding of vocabulary and spelling concepts, make individual student copies and have each student explain in writing his thought process for answering each problem.

CONTEXT CLUES

Explain the meaning of the boldfaced word in the sentence below. Then write a sentence that answers the question.

Why was Monica so **reticent** during lunch today?

1

CONTEXT CLUES

What word rhymes with *thaw* and makes a phrase that begins with *last*?

2

CONTEXT CLUES

Which word below best completes the sentence?

My sister is a very _____ writer. She finished ten beautiful poems in just two days.

A. sluggish
B. perplexed
C. fluent

3

CONTEXT CLUES

Rearrange the letters in the boldfaced word in the sentence below to spell another word that completes the sentence.

I need to clean the **study** because it is very _____.

4

CONTEXT CLUES

Find the mistakes in the sentence below.

Their are fore errers in this passage. Read carfully to see if you can find all of them.

5

BONUS BUILDER #1

Where does each number belong?

A newspaper sold _____ more newspapers this year than in _____. About _____ percent of the paper's _____ new readers like the front page best. Only _____ percent prefer the comics.

54   1990   600   16   1,200

CONTEXT CLUES

©2001 The Education Center, Inc. • *Mind Builders* Vocabulary & Spelling • TEC1610 • Key p. 44

CONTEXT CLUES

Todd's grandmother phoned to say she is bringing him a special gift. The phone connection was poor, so he couldn't hear what the gift is. Todd thinks it is one of the items below. Which one makes the most sense?

    A. concussion
    B. confection
    C. coronation

6

CONTEXT CLUES

List three words that could complete the sentence below in a sensible way.

Judy tried very hard to get the _____ open, but it would not budge.

7

CONTEXT CLUES

Pear is to *fruit* as *beef* is to _____.

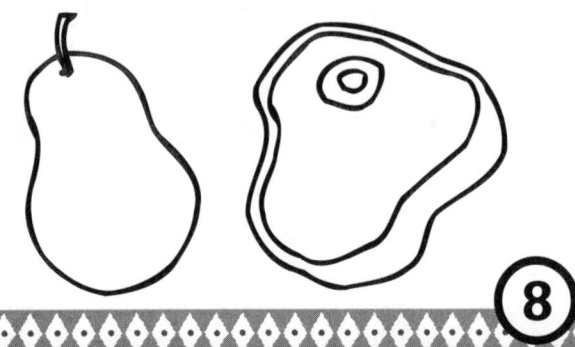

8

CONTEXT CLUES

Rewrite the sentence below as a simple, well-known proverb.

During the feline's absence, the multiple rodents will engage in folly.

9

CONTEXT CLUES

Change one letter in the boldfaced word below to make the sentence make sense.

The talented artist painted a colorful **moral** on the wall.

10

BONUS BUILDER #2

Rearrange the same six letters to make three different words that complete the sentence below.

The _ _ _ _ _ _-colored _ _ _ _ _ _ , together with the red rose _ _ _ _ _ _ , make the dinner table look beautiful.

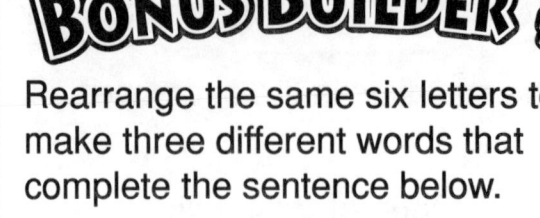

CONTEXT CLUES

CONTEXT CLUES

List three color words that are commonly grouped together and that each rhyme with one of the following words: *fed, fright, flew*.

(11)

CONTEXT CLUES

Which word below would *not* make sense in this sentence?

The law _____ that a person obtain a driver's license before driving a car.

A. requires B. compensates
C. insists   D. demands

(12)

CONTEXT CLUES

Use the same five letters to make two different words that can complete the sentence below.

It's too _____ to put on the second _____ of paint.

(13)

CONTEXT CLUES

What baseball word also applies to music?

(14)

CONTEXT CLUES

What is the meaning of the boldfaced word in the sentence below? Write a sentence that answers the question.

Who tried to **usurp** the president's authority?

(15)

BONUS BUILDER #3

Write the word that matches each definition below. Then identify the three-letter animal word contained in each answer.

A. to trap something with the hands
B. tomato sauce for french fries
C. a short sleep
D. a book that lists a company's products
E. a great and sudden disaster

CONTEXT CLUES

CONTEXT CLUES

Rewrite the sentence below as a simple, well-known proverb.

Make fodder during the time that the star around which the earth orbits radiates light.

16

CONTEXT CLUES

Use the same four letters to make two different words that complete the sentence below.

I _____ dropped an entire ice-cream _____ .

17

CONTEXT CLUES

What word rhymes with *walk* and combines with *board* to make a compound word that names something found in a classroom?

__?__ + __?__ = _____?_____

18

CONTEXT CLUES

Change one letter in the boldfaced word below to make the sentence make sense.

A pebble became **dodged** in my shoe, and I couldn't pull it out.

19

CONTEXT CLUES

What one word fits in all three blanks of the sentence below? Give two different answers.

Betsy _____ and _____ and _____, but still she could not reach her brother.

20

BONUS BUILDER #4

Rearrange the boldfaced words so that the paragraph makes sense.

On **dogcatcher** day, a 20-year-old **position** student and a 60-year-old **college** were both running for the **doctor** of county **election. Win** wondered why these candidates wanted the **everyone** and which person would **job**.

CONTEXT CLUES

CONTEXT CLUES

Choose the word that best completes the sentence below.

Because I didn't ____ my friend's warning, I stepped on the ice patch and fell flat on my back.

A. heed   B. beckon   C. impede

(21)

CONTEXT CLUES

List at least seven three-letter words that name parts of the body.

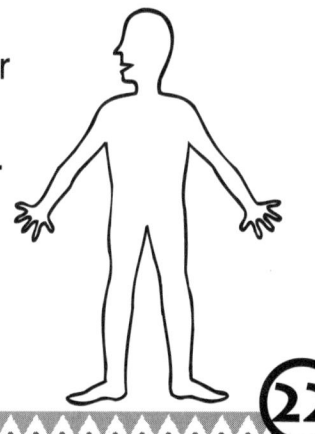

(22)

CONTEXT CLUES

In a letter, Steve learns that his uncle is bringing him a gift when he visits. But the uncle's handwriting is so bad, Steve can't tell what the gift is. It could be one of the items below. Which one makes the most sense?

A. scabies   B. sardines   C. sweets

(23)

CONTEXT CLUES

Square is to *shape* as *red* is to _____.

(24)

CONTEXT CLUES

Rearrange the letters of one word in the sentence below to make a word that best completes the sentence.

Grandpa's apples have the best taste in the whole _____.

(25)

BONUS BUILDER #5

Divide the letters of the boldfaced word below to form new words that complete the sentence.

Because there was ____ ____ in the operating room, the **notable** surgeon was ____ ____ to perform surgery.

CONTEXT CLUES

CONTEXT CLUES

Change one letter of one word to make the sentence below make sense.

Our family is hoping to spend Christmas at a ski report.

26

CONTEXT CLUES

What is the meaning of the boldfaced word in the sentence below? Write a sentence that answers the question.

What is the **sleuth** trying to find?

27

CONTEXT CLUES

List three seasonal words that belong together and that each rhyme with one of the following words: *ring, drummer, haul.*

28

CONTEXT CLUES

What word could complete the sentence below? Give three different answers.

It is clear that Bryce is very _____ because he has made so many interesting gadgets.

29

CONTEXT CLUES

Rewrite the sentence below as a simple, well-known proverb.

Refrain from enumerating your fowl prior to when they emerge from the eggs.

30

BONUS BUILDER #6

If the word *waputts* means *pets* in the sentences below, what could *pnifs, pnufs,* and *valooms* be?

The Galoopalias wanted only pnifs and pnufs as waputts. They had no use for valooms as waputts.

CONTEXT CLUES

CONTEXT CLUES

Melanie accidentally splashed water on the note listing the items she needs for a project. Help Melanie figure out the unreadable words.

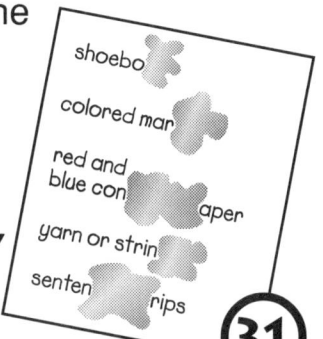

31

CONTEXT CLUES

Complete the analogy below.

Tree is to *lumber* as *wheat* is to _____.

32

CONTEXT CLUES

What words best complete the rhyme below?

Stan's friends have thought of him as a whiz kid
Ever since he _____.

 33

CONTEXT CLUES

Erica left the items listed below on a table. Based on these items, what had Erica been doing?

colorful paper scraps, scissors, glue, colorful pens and markers, newspaper clippings, ticket stubs, photographs, mementos

 34

CONTEXT CLUES

Rewrite the sentence below as a simple, well-known proverb.

A pair of pates is much preferred to a single noggin.

 35

BONUS BUILDER #7

Where does each word below fit in the paragraph?

Samantha frowned. She didn't agree with Duncan's _____. She wanted to _____ before they left for the stadium. It was _____ now, and it'd be _____ before they arrived. _____ Samantha packed a _____.

So   decision   eat   7 P.M.   snack   5 P.M.

CONTEXT CLUES

Synonyms & Antonyms

What two antonyms are woven together below? (Do not change the order of any letters.)

r a s p l i o w d

(36)

Synonyms & Antonyms

Which word below does not mean the same as the others?

glow   blaze   blend   gleam

(37)

Synonyms & Antonyms

Which word below is not a synonym for *eat*?

nibble   munch   relish
dine   consume

(38)

Synonyms & Antonyms

List as many words as you can that are synonyms for *hard*.

(39)

Synonyms & Antonyms

Change *east* to *west* in three steps. Do this by changing one letter in *east* at a time to a different letter.

east
_ _ _ _
_ _ _ _
west

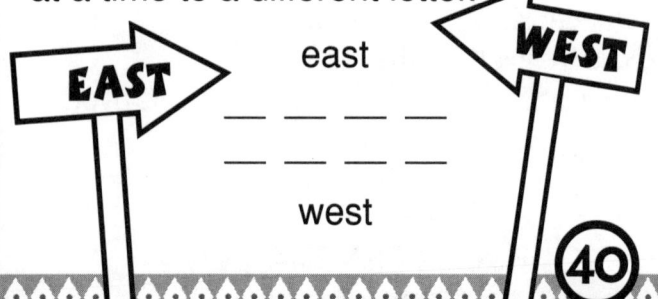

(40)

Bonus Builder #8

Complete this magic word square by writing a synonym for each clue below. The words going down and across are the same.

1. nuisance
2. sound repetition
3. display
4. village

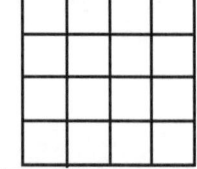

Synonyms & Antonyms

Synonyms & Antonyms

Write two five-letter words that mean "tiny spot" and end in the same three letters.

(41)

Synonyms & Antonyms

Replace one word in each nonsense compound word below with its antonym to spell a real word.

catsdown   nooff

(42)

Synonyms & Antonyms

Write a synonym for the verb *make* that starts with each letter below.

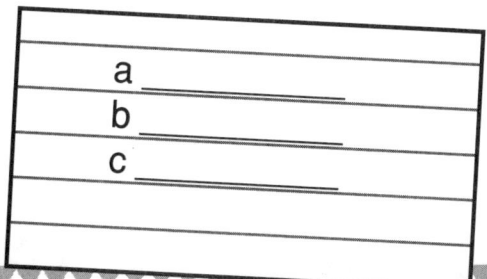

a _____
b _____
c _____

(43)

Synonyms & Antonyms

Change each set of words below into a pair of synonyms by moving one letter from the first word to the second word.

curt–cave   flat–pump

(44)

Synonyms & Antonyms

Unscramble the letters below to make a pair of antonyms.

eleasp–weaka

(45)

Bonus Builder #9

Write an *oxymoron,* a two-word antonym phrase, for each description below.

A. weighty lantern
B. not many parcels of land
C. lowermost spinning toy

Synonyms & Antonyms

Synonyms & Antonyms

What word is a synonym for both *hair* and *fasteners*?

46

Synonyms & Antonyms

Which two words below have opposite meanings?

47

Synonyms & Antonyms

For each word below, write a synonym that begins with *u.*

  A. overturn
  B. comprehend
  C. futile

48

Synonyms & Antonyms

What two antonyms are woven together below? (Do not change the order of any letters.)

s r o m o u g o h t h

49

Synonyms & Antonyms

Write a synonym for each word below. All of the synonyms should rhyme.

  A. snatch   B. chatter   C. dull

50

Bonus Builder #10

Find a short word within each longer word below that is a synonym (or a near synonym) for the longer word. For example, **curt**ail–**cut.** Use your dictionary for help.

  A. feasts   B. observe   C. separate
  D. latest   E. instructor

Synonyms & Antonyms

Synonyms & Antonyms

Change *sick* to its antonym *well* in four steps by changing one letter at a time to form a different word.

sick
_ _ _ _
_ _ _ _
_ _ _ _
well

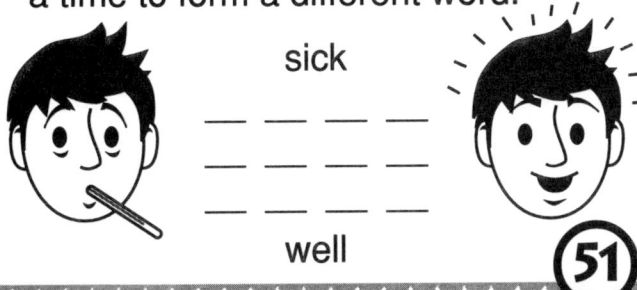

51

Synonyms & Antonyms

Which word below does not have the same meaning as the others?

weak   stiff   feeble   frail

52

Synonyms & Antonyms

Write a synonym for the verb *tie* that begins with each letter below.

b_____
f _____
k _____

53

Synonyms & Antonyms

Replace one word in each nonsense compound word below with its antonym to form a real compound word.

outhabit   againstgive

54

Synonyms & Antonyms

Write two nonrhyming five-letter words that end in the same three letters and mean "to give instruction to."

55

Bonus Builder #11

Use the letters in *gasoline* to write a pair of antonyms.

Synonyms & Antonyms

©2001 The Education Center, Inc. • Mind Builders • Vocabulary & Spelling • TEC1610 • Key p. 45

Synonyms & Antonyms

Change each set of words below into a pair of synonyms by moving one letter from the first word to the second word.

scarer–fight
ripe–tar

56

Synonyms & Antonyms

The word *tight* can sometimes be a synonym for *tricky*. Write a sentence in which *tight* is used in this way.

57

Synonyms & Antonyms

Which two words below are synonyms?

jovial   sullen   glum   pure

58

Synonyms & Antonyms

Write a four-letter word that means "shawl" or "coat." Then rearrange the four letters to make a word that means to "twist out of shape."

59

Synonyms & Antonyms

Write a five-letter word that is similar in meaning to *after* and contains four of the same letters.

60

Bonus Builder #12

Complete this crossword by using the boxes to spell synonyms for *happy*.

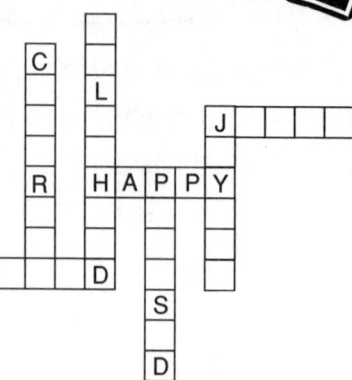

Synonyms & Antonyms

Synonyms & Antonyms

What letters are needed below to spell a synonym for *event*?

o __ __ u __ __ en __ __

61

Synonyms & Antonyms

Identify the two antonyms that are woven together below. (Do not change the order of any letters.)

s n i l o e n i s t y

62

Synonyms & Antonyms

What word is a synonym for both *shape* and *calculate*?

63

Synonyms & Antonyms

Replace a word in each nonsense compound word below with its antonym to form a real word.

losesome   blackin

64

Synonyms & Antonyms

Change *give* to its antonym *take* in four steps by changing one letter at a time to form a different word.

give
— — — —
— — — —
— — — —
take

65

Bonus Builder #13

Look at the puzzle. Begin at Start. Move one box in any direction to spell two ten-letter synonyms for *responsibility*. Circle the first letter of the second word.

START			
O	B	L	M
G	I	C	M	I
T	A	N	M	T
I	O	E	N	T

STOP

Synonyms & Antonyms

Synonyms & Antonyms

What two antonyms are woven together below? (Do not change the order of any letters.)

l d i a g r h k t

(66)

Synonyms & Antonyms

Which word below does not mean the same as the others?

(67)

Synonyms & Antonyms

Write a synonym for the verb *give* that starts with each letter below.

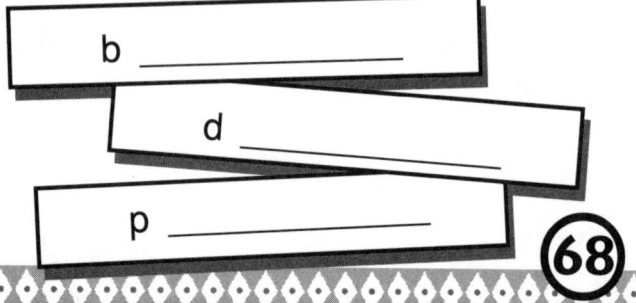

(68)

Synonyms & Antonyms

Unscramble the letters below to form a pair of antonyms.

g c n i a t g i – r e n i m a u t i

(69)

Synonyms & Antonyms

Write a synonym for each word below. All of the synonyms should rhyme.

A. pile   B. hit   C. follow   D. talk

(70)

Bonus Builder #14

Rematch the words in the pairs below to form two pairs of synonyms and two pairs of antonyms.

peak–support   resolve–crest
settle–descend   oppose–soar

Synonyms & Antonyms

Homophones

Rewrite the sentence below, replacing each incorrect homophone with the correct one.

   I due knot no which shirt two chews: the read won or the blew one.

(71)

Homophones

Write the homophone pairs that match the definitions below.

   A. an amphibian, pulled with a rope
   B. a vegetable, a unit of weight used to measure precious stones

(72)

Homophones

An *anagram* is a word made by changing the order of the letters of another word. For example, changing *late* to *tale*. List as many pairs of anagram homophones as you can.

(73)

Homophones

Write the pair of homophones that completes the sentence below.

   After we paint the _____, we will be _____ the wall paneling with wax.

(74)

Homophones

Which words in the homophone pairs below are musical instruments? Units of money?

symbol–cymbal
sent–cent
lyre–liar

(75)

Bonus Builder #15

List one homophone pair for at least 20 different letters of the alphabet. At least one word in each pair must begin with each letter. For example, A—air–Heir and B—bare–bear. Do not repeat any words.

Homophones

Homophones

Find the pair of homophones hidden in the sentence below.

With early care, he really should not need surgery.

(76)

Homophones

Which homophone in each pair is correct in the sentence below?

Little Louis is not yet (allowed–aloud) to eat pickled (beats–beets).

(77)

Homophones

List four sets of homophones that include number words.

(78)

Homophones

Start with *groan*. Remove one letter at a time to form a new word, rearranging the letters if needed, until you have the letter *a*. Then start with the letter *o*. Add one letter at a time to form a new word, rearranging the letters if needed, until you spell the word *grown*.

groan   o
___   ___
___   ___
___   ___
a   grown

(79)

Homophones

Write the homophone pair that matches the definitions below.

boyfriend–a decorative knot

(80)

Bonus Builder #16

List as many homophone pairs as you can that rhyme with *hair–hare*.

Homophones

HOMOPHONES

Write a sentence using the homophone pair *pale–pail* correctly.

(81)

HOMOPHONES

List as many homophone pairs as you can whose words start with different letters.

(82)

HOMOPHONES

Rewrite the sentence below, replacing each incorrect homophone with the correct one.

Their was a brief paws before she maid the decision to higher a knew mechanic to fix her car's breaks.

(83)

HOMOPHONES

Write the homophone pair that matches the definitions below.

A. several musical notes played together–a thin rope
B. a kind of tree–soft, thick animal hair

(84)

HOMOPHONES

Write the homophone pair that completes the sentence below.

The dog buried the _____ set of bones in a single _____.

(85)

Bonus Builder #17

Write a sentence that includes three or more homophone pairs.

HOMOPHONES

Homophones

What homophone pair is in the answer to the riddle below?

How can you shape a pear to make it look like an apple?

(86)

Homophones

Which homophones below name tools? Which ones can be used to write a letter?

ax   all   acts
stationary   awl   stationery

(87)

Homophones

List two homophone pairs in which one word in each pair ends in *x*.

(88)

Homophones

Write a sentence using the homophone pair *great–grate* correctly.

(89)

Homophones

Write the homophone pair that completes the sentence below.

Because of the heavy _____, the driver _____ the turn and got lost.

(90)

Bonus Builder #18

How many words in the box have homophones? List them.

rote	away
picture	ball
wring	creak
bide	sow

Homophones

Homophones

Which homophone in each pair is correct in the sentence below?

The (principle–principal) heard the teacher say, "Every sentence should begin with a (capital–capitol) letter."

91

Homophones

Answer the riddle below using a sentence that contains two homophone pairs.

What is the difference between a man who has been to Niagara Falls and one who has not?

92

Homophones

Rewrite the sentence below, replacing each incorrect homophone with the correct one.

He guest that Paul's party wood bee a grate won.

93

Homophones

List a homophone pair that sounds like each of the following letters of the alphabet: *b, c, o,* and *t.*

94

Homophones

Write a homophone pair that completes the sentence below.

If the leftover sweets go to _____, they won't go to your _____.

95

Bonus Builder #19

List as many sets of three homophones, such as *there–their–they're,* as you can.

Homophones

Homophones

Find the homophone pair that is hidden in the sentence below.

Nick will travel to Spain soon, and he hopes to go to Japan eventually.

96

Homophones

Unscramble the letters below to make a familiar homophone pair.

seon–skonw

97

Homophones

Write a homophone pair that matches the definitions below.

a quick look–the top of a mountain

98

Homophones

Write a riddle that contains any homophone pair.

99

Homophones

List as many sets of homophones that contain proper nouns as you can.

100

Bonus Builder #20

Start with *waist*. Remove one letter at a time to form a new word, rearranging the letters if needed, until you form the word *I*. Then start with the word *a*. Add one letter at a time to form a new word, rearranging the letters if needed, until you spell the word *waste*.

waist   a
___   ___
___   ___
___   ___
I   waste

Homophones

©2001 The Education Center, Inc. • Mind Builders • Vocabulary & Spelling • TEC1610 • Key p. 46

Homophones

Which words in the homophone pairs below are persons? Things you can buy?

assistance–assistants
beau–bow
boarder–border
marshal–martial
none–nun
profit–prophet
attendance–attendants
bell–belle
knight–night
friar–fryer
patience–patients
serf–surf

101

Homophones

Write the homophone pairs that match the definitions below.

A. a small raisin–the fast part of a stream
B. a military rank–a grain of corn

102

Homophones

List as many homophone pairs as you can in which one word in the pair names a food.

103

Homophones

Write a sentence containing the homophone pair *shear–sheer*.

104

Homophones

Write a sentence using the homophone pair *who's–whose* correctly.

105

Bonus Builder #21

Write two homophones for each word below.

I'll   I   you   he'll   we'll

Homophones

Prefixes & Suffixes

List eight action verbs that require the last letter to be doubled before adding a suffix such as -ed or -ing.

dd   tt   mm   pp   rr

106

Prefixes & Suffixes

Write a word ending in -ent for each clue below.

A. one who is in charge

B. one who lives in a particular place

C. one who receives

107

Prefixes & Suffixes

What are two different two-letter prefixes that can be used in the blanks below to form a word?

__ __clude

108

Prefixes & Suffixes

Identify the occupation, or job, in which a person does the following:

A. writes biographies

B. performs manicures

C. studies astronomy

109

Prefixes & Suffixes

How many sides does a *hex*agonal table have? An *oct*agonal table? A *tri*angular table?

110

Bonus Builder #22

Form as many words from the prefixes, suffixes, and base words below as you can.

Prefixes: *re-, un-, mis-*
Suffixes: *-ed, -ing*
Base Words: *match, test, pack*

Prefixes & Suffixes

Prefixes & Suffixes

What one prefix can be added to all of the words below?

111

Prefixes & Suffixes

If one word's suffix in the sentence below is changed, then the sentence has the opposite meaning. What is the word? What is the new suffix?

It is clearly useful to keep cleaning the garage.

112

Prefixes & Suffixes

List eight action verbs that do not require the last letter to be doubled before adding a suffix such as *-ed* or *-ing*.

113

Prefixes & Suffixes

Write a four-letter word to which both a prefix and a suffix can be added. Use this word in a sentence.

114

Prefixes & Suffixes

Write a word containing a prefix that matches each definition below.

   A. not able to be moved
   B. not legal
   C. not fed enough

115

Bonus Builder #23

Use all the letters in the words on each card below to form a different ten-letter word that contains a common suffix.

A. sip, sat, lice

B. odd, all, neck

C. sun, pin, them

Prefixes & Suffixes

Prefixes & Suffixes

What words that are units of weight when standing alone can be used with the prefix *pro-* to form three new words?

(116)

Prefixes & Suffixes

List at least four prefixes that mean "not."

(117)

Prefixes & Suffixes

Which word in parentheses is correct in the sentence below?

We are all (hoping, hopping) to find out where the pilot will be (fling, flying) tomorrow.

(118)

Prefixes & Suffixes

What form of the boldfaced word below best completes the following sentence?

The little boy is **happy** on his birthday than on any other day of the year.

(119)

Prefixes & Suffixes

To which word(s) below can the prefix *mis-* be added?

break   behave   conduct
fortune   out

(120)

Bonus Builder #24

Using the letters in *mistakable* in order, form as many words of four or more letters as you can. *Make* could be one of the words because *a* follows *m*, *k* follows *a*, and *e* follows *k*. *Bake* could not be one of the words because *b* comes after *a*.

Prefixes & Suffixes

Prefixes & Suffixes

To which of the rhyming words below can the suffix *-ing* be added?

121

Prefixes & Suffixes

Write a five-letter word to which both a prefix and a suffix can be added. Use this word in a sentence.

prefix + XXXXX + suffix
        word

122

Prefixes & Suffixes

What occupation ending with the suffix *-er* contains three sets of double letters?

123

Prefixes & Suffixes

When the suffix *-th* is added to *hundredth*, the spelling of the base word does not change. Write four words in which the spelling of the base word *does* change when adding *-th*.

124

Prefixes & Suffixes

Use all ten letters in *thousandth* to form three words of three to four letters each.

125

Bonus Builder #25

List at least 20 words to which the prefix *dis-* can be added.

Prefixes & Suffixes

Prefixes & Suffixes

A family has four *bi*cycles, three *tri*cycles, and one *uni*cycle. How many wheels are there in all?

126

Prefixes & Suffixes

Unscramble the letters below to spell a word that has a three-letter suffix.

e g r u f f o l t

127

Prefixes & Suffixes

What form of the boldfaced word below best completes the following sentence?

Due to the heavy snowfall, it is **doubt** that there will be school tomorrow.

128

Prefixes & Suffixes

What five-letter prefix means "below" or "beneath?"

129

Prefixes & Suffixes

If someone can't **decide** where to put his coat, then he is _____.

130

Bonus Builder #26

Add *ee*, *ff*, *ll*, or *ss* to each word below to form an eight-letter word containing a suffix. For example, adding *ff* to *ruling* forms *ruffling*.

A. needle   B. string   C. exceed

Prefixes & Suffixes

Prefixes & Suffixes

Name the occupation, or job, in which a person does the following:

A. edits books or magazines

B. sews

C. draws cartoons

131

Prefixes & Suffixes

What suffix can be added to the following words without requiring a change in spelling?

elect   product   subject

132

Prefixes & Suffixes

Write a word that contains both a prefix and a suffix to match each definition below.

A. not able to be reversed
B. not able to be denied
C. sized too large

133

Prefixes & Suffixes

How many different two-letter prefixes can be used with the word below?

____ cover

134

Prefixes & Suffixes

Write a six-letter base word to which both a prefix and a suffix have been added.

135

Bonus Builder #27

Look at the word below. Its base word *start* has the same number of letters as its prefix and suffix combined (five). Write three more words that follow this pattern. Use words that contain a prefix, a suffix, or both.

re*start*ing

Prefixes & Suffixes

Prefixes & Suffixes

Write a word containing a prefix that matches each definition below.

  A. among or between nations
  B. a self-written life story
  C. half of a sphere

(136)

Prefixes & Suffixes

The prefixes below describe size. Write three words, one for each prefix. Then explain in your own words what each word means.

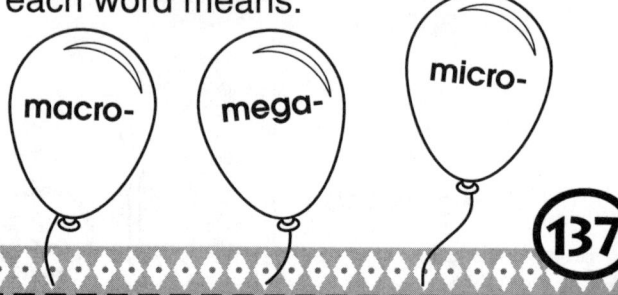

(137)

Prefixes & Suffixes

Change each word below to an adjective by adding one of the following suffixes: -ic, -ed, -ous, -ative, -y, and -en. Remember: The spelling of some base words might need to change!

talk	earth	bake
danger	sun	joy	metal

(138)

Prefixes & Suffixes

List at least five words containing suffixes that have to do with the *state* or *quality of* something, such as hero*ism* and happi*ness*.

(139)

Prefixes & Suffixes

Add the suffix -ation to each word below. Which word did *not* need a change of spelling?

  narrate   compute   visit   sum
  declare   recite   vocalize

(140)

Bonus Builder #28

List at least ten words containing prefixes that mean "after" or "before."

Prefixes & Suffixes

Word Origins

Bus is the shortened form of a longer word. Unscramble the letters below to form the longer word.

o b s u n i m

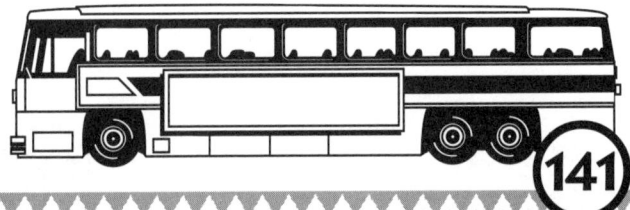

141

Word Origins

What is *melba toast?* For whom was it named? What other food bears this person's name?

142

Word Origins

What four-letter word has both of the meanings below? Hint: The word comes from the Latin words *solea* (sandal) and *solum* (bottom).

a kind of fish, the bottom of a foot or shoe

143

Word Origins

An *acronym* is a shortened word formed by combining the first letters or syllables of a string of words. *Radar* is an acronym. What words do its letters represent?

144

Word Origins

The Latin word *manus* means "hand." List three words beginning with *man-* that refer to things done with or to the hands. What does each word mean?

145

Bonus Builder #29

Separate the letters below to form two words of French origin. One comes from a French word meaning "little forest." The other comes from a French word that means "hook."

c b r o o c u h q e u t e t

Word Origins

©2001 The Education Center, Inc. • Mind Builders Vocabulary & Spelling • TEC1610 • Key p. 47   31

Word Origins

What two rhyming words of French origin match the definitions below?

A. a light, flowing dance

B. a hut (or cottage) in the Alps

146

Word Origins

List three words that come from the Latin word *audire* (to hear).

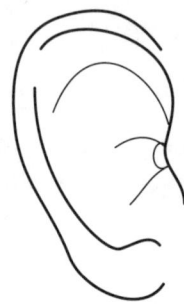

147

Word Origins

What two words were combined to make the word *smog?*

148

Word Origins

What dance from the 1920s is named after the city in which it began?

149

Word Origins

What are *bloomers?* For whom were they named?

150

Bonus Builder #30

A *spoonerism* is a word or phrase in which key sounds are switched. For example, *Don't count your hickens before they're chatched.* The spoonerism is named after Archibald Spooner, who frequently misspoke in this way. Rewrite each saying below as a spoonerism.

Don't cry over spilled milk.

Still waters run deep.

Word Origins

WORD ORIGINS

There was a popular television show many years ago called *M*A*S*H*. What words do these letters represent?

(151)

WORD ORIGINS

Which line below looks longer? Actually, both lines are the same length! They represent an *optical* illusion. What is the origin of the word *optical*?

(152)

WORD ORIGINS

What common illness is the shortened form of a longer word without its beginning and ending? Write both the long and short forms of this word.

(153)

WORD ORIGINS

What six-letter word from a French word meaning "desk" matches both of the definitions below?

a low chest of drawers   a government department

(154)

WORD ORIGINS

What nine-letter word named after Tangier, Morocco, is a tasty way of getting vitamin C?

(155)

Bonus Builder #31

Many words in the fields of science and medicine are named after people who made important discoveries. Identify the person for whom each word below was named.

A. decibel   B. salmonella
C. pasteurization   D. volt
E. watt

WORD ORIGINS

©2001 The Education Center, Inc. • *Mind Builders • Vocabulary & Spelling* • TEC1610 • Key p. 47   33

Word Origins

Write two words that originate from the Greek root *scop* (see).

156

Word Origins

Back in the 1800s, Ambrose Burnside wore whiskers in front of his ears. What one of these whiskers is called today is an *anagram* (a rearrangement of letters) of his last name. What is it called?

157

Word Origins

What two words were combined to form the word *brunch*?

158

Word Origins

What French phrase is often used to wish someone well just before they go on a long journey?

159

Word Origins

A popular card game got its name from the Spanish word for *one*. If a new game were named for the Spanish word for *two*, what would it be called?

160

Bonus Builder #32

Write the words that represent each well-known acronym below.

A. ZIP (as in *ZIP* code)
B. UNICEF
C. ROTC
D. SUNOCO
E. NASCAR

Word Origins

Word Origins

Unscramble the word of French origin below that names someone who drives a car for pay.

f r a c e h u f u

161

Word Origins

People who use an automatic banking machine need a bank card and a *PIN*. What is a *PIN*?

162

Word Origins

The Latin word *foras* means "outside." What word of this origin describes a person visiting from another country?

163

Word Origins

Write the names of three flowers that have been named after people.

164

Word Origins

What are two six-letter Spanish words whose spellings are the same except for the first letters? Hint: One word means "holiday or festival." The other means "afternoon rest."

165

Bonus Builder #33

In the poem "Jabberwocky," Lewis Carroll combined familiar words to form funny new words. For example, he combined *gallop* and *triumph* to form *galumph* and *chuckle* and *snort* to form *chortle*. Use this method to invent five new words of your own.

Word Origins

WORD ORIGINS

What familiar word comes from the German words that mean "a garden of children"?

166

WORD ORIGINS

For whom was the teddy bear named?

167

WORD ORIGINS

Unscramble the word below that means "an answer to a problem." It comes from a Latin word meaning "to loosen."

t u s n o l o i

168

WORD ORIGINS

Write two words that were formed from the Latin root *sign* (mark).

169

WORD ORIGINS

What word from the Latin root *clud* means "to end"?

170

Bonus Builder #34

The Greek word *phobos* means "fear." Identify the fear associated with each word below.

A. ailurophobia
B. acrophobia
C. claustrophobia
D. anthropophobia
E. ornithophobia

WORD ORIGINS

WORD ORIGINS

The Latin words *et cetera* mean "and others." Use this expression's three-letter abbreviation in a sentence.

(171)

WORD ORIGINS

Some months of the year were named after Roman gods or goddesses. Write the name of the god or goddess and the corresponding month of the year that matches each clue below.

A. the god with two faces, one looking forward and the other looking backward
B. the god of war
C. the goddess who was the mother of Mercury

WORD ORIGINS

What word does each letter in the acronyms below stand for?

Order a BLT sandwich for me ASAP!

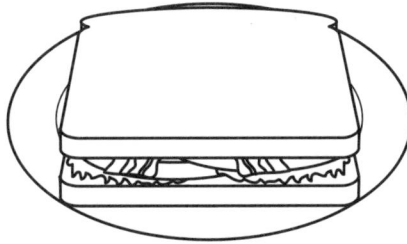

(173)

WORD ORIGINS

What words were combined to form each word below?

A. telethon
B. pixel
C. travelogue
D. motocross
E. splatter

WORD ORIGINS

Each group of scrambled letters below is the shortened form of a word. Write both the long and short forms of each word. Then use any two of the short forms in a sentence.

A. poyt
B. tve
C. oilm
D. gefird

Bonus Builder #35

Sometimes new words are formed by joining two words together to form *compound words.* See how many compound words you can list that contain at least one of the words below.

WORD ORIGINS

Figures of Speech

An *idiom* is an expression that means something other than the usual meaning of the words. Replace one word in each expression below with its antonym (or near antonym) to make a familiar idiom.

A. We're in cold water now!
B. You're pulling my arm!
C. Let's just uncover the hatchet.

(176)

Figures of Speech

What familiar idiom is illustrated below? What does it mean?

READING

(177)

Figures of Speech

A *metaphor* compares two unlike things directly, as in the statement "His arms are pillars." Write a metaphor of your own about one of the following objects: a jigsaw puzzle, gumdrops, scissors, an envelope, or a hammer.

(178)

Figures of Speech

Complete each figurative expression below with the name of a different body part.

A. keep a straight _____
B. turn a cold _____
C. keep your _____ on straight

(179)

Figures of Speech

Unscramble the letters below to discover the name of the figure of speech that is an exaggerated comparison.

b o p l y e h e r

(180)

Bonus Builder #36

Describe what a picture representing a literal interpretation of each idiomatic expression below would show.

A. It's raining cats and dogs.
B. The boss is over a barrel on this one.
C. I heard it straight from the horse's mouth.

Figures of Speech

Figures of Speech

What one word completes all three sentences below? Explain what each sentence means.

A. Everyone has to _____ his own weight around here.
B. We weren't sure we'd be able to _____ off that performance.
C. His dad can _____ some strings to help him get a job.

(181)

Figures of Speech

Explain the difference between a *simile* and a *metaphor*.

(182)

Figures of Speech

Write as many idioms that include the word *eat* as you can.

(183)

Figures of Speech

Complete each simile below in a different, creative way.

A. ate like _____
B. walked like _____
C. shone like _____

(184)

Figures of Speech

Write a synonym for each boldfaced word or phrase below to make a familiar simile.

as **jolly** as **a brown songbird**

(185)

Bonus Builder #37

Many idiomatic expressions include items of clothing. For example, "Megan has a *bee in her bonnet* about cleaning her room." Write three idioms that include articles of clothing. Explain the meaning of each one.

Figures of Speech

Figures of Speech

Complete the simile below by using a word that accurately describes yourself in some way.

My friends wish they were as _____ as I am.

186

Figures of Speech

Write a sentence in which a goldfish has a human quality.

187

Figures of Speech

What familiar idiom is illustrated below?

188

Figures of Speech

Write one or more figurative expressions for each color word below.

A. green   B. blue   C. red

189

Figures of Speech

Write three idiomatic expressions that mean someone is upset or unhappy. Then use each expression in a different sentence.

190

Bonus Builder #38

Decode the idiom below using a special code. Find each letter on a computer keyboard. Replace each letter with the letter directly to its left.

o   jsbr   s   npmr   yp
[ovl   eoyj   upi!

Figures of Speech

Figures of Speech

Complete each expression below with the name of a different animal.
 A. If you're wrong, you'll have to eat _____.
 B. We can really ___ out at the party!
 C. That project, unfortunately, is going to the _____.

(191)

Figures of Speech

Pretend that a patch of grass can talk. Write three sentences—each one containing a different figure of speech—to express what the grass might say.

(192)

Figures of Speech

Rearrange the words below so they make a goofy play on words related to the weather.

| won't | rain | it | down | if |
| keeps | this | up | come | |

(193)

Figures of Speech

Complete the sentence below so that it makes an exaggeration.

  Mary Lynn was so excited she _____.

(194)

Figures of Speech

A *metaphor* compares two unlike things directly. For example, "Her eyes were pools of water." Write a metaphor of your own that includes one of the following objects: a tree, icing, sunshine, a bracelet, or a book.

(195)

Bonus Builder #39

American tall tales are great sources of figurative language, especially exaggeration! Remember Paul Bunyan and John Henry? Write three sentences in which you exaggerate about your favorite tall-tale character meeting someone (or something) who is either *very* large or *very* small.

Figures of Speech

Figures of Speech

Complete each simile below in a different, creative way.

A. heavy as _____
B. light as _____
C. clear as _____

196

Figures of Speech

Complete each figurative expression below with a different color word. Explain the meaning of each expression.

A. Every cloud has a _____ lining.
B. Uncle Eddie has a heart of _____.
C. The big announcement came out of the _____.

197

Figures of Speech

What familiar expression is illustrated below?

4 5 6 S A F E T Y 7 8 9

198

Figures of Speech

What one word completes both sentences below?

A. We'll have to be careful how we _____ the news to Joe.
B. Do not _____ your word to your parents.

199

Figures of Speech

Write as many idioms that include the word *throw* as you can.

200

Bonus Builder #40

Many idiomatic phrases include musical terms or instruments, such as *harping on a subject* or *having an upbeat attitude*. Write three idioms that include musical terms or instruments. Explain the meaning of each one.

Figures of Speech

Figures of Speech

Complete the sentence below so that it makes an exaggeration.

Derek was so cold he _____.

201

Figures of Speech

Write a sentence in which a rock has a human quality.

202

Figures of Speech

Complete each figurative expression below with the name of a different body part.
- A. turn a deaf _____
- B. keep an _____ on it
- C. get in someone's _____

203

Figures of Speech

Write a synonym for each boldfaced word below to make a familiar idiom. Explain what the idiom means. Then use it in a sentence.

capture the **dessert**

204

Figures of Speech

Complete the simile below using a word that accurately describes your best friend in some way.

All friends should be as _____ as mine.

205

Bonus Builder #41

Many similes include the names of animals, such as *fat as a pig*. Write as many similes as you can that include the names of animals. Then write three sentences, using a different simile in each sentence.

Figures of Speech

Answer Keys

Page 3
1. In the sentence provided, *reticent* means *not inclined to talk*. Possible sentence to answer the question: Monica was *reticent* during lunch because her stomach hurt.
2. straw
3. C. fluent
4. dusty
5. The mistakes are misspellings: *there, four, errors,* and *carefully*.

Bonus Builder #1: A newspaper sold **1,200** more newspapers this year than in **1990**. About **54** percent of the paper's **600** new readers like the front page best. Only **16** percent prefer the comics.

Page 4
6. B. confection
7. Students' answers may vary. Possible answers include *door, handle, lock,* and *zipper.*
8. meat
9. When the cat's away, the mice will play.
10. mural

Bonus Builder #2: The **pastel**-colored **plates,** together with the red rose **petals,** make the dinner table look beautiful.

Page 5
11. red, white, blue
12. B. compensates
13. early, layer
14. Students' answers will vary. Possible answers include *run, pitch, slide,* and *score.*
15. *Usurp* means to wrongfully seize or assume power. Students' sentences will vary. Possible sentence: The president's cabinet tried to usurp the president's authority.

Bonus Builder #3: A. catch, B. catsup, C. catnap, D. catalog, E. catastrophe
Animal: cat

Page 6
16. Make hay while the sun shines.
17. once, cone
18. chalk
19. lodged
20. Students' answers will vary. Possible answers include *tried, phoned, ran, worked,* and *stretched.*

Bonus Builder #4: On **election** day, a 20-year-old **college** student and a 60-year-old **doctor** were both running for the **position** of county **dogcatcher. Everyone** wondered why these candidates wanted the **job** and which person would **win.**

Page 7
21. A. heed
22. Students' answers will vary. Possible answers include *eye, ear, lip, leg, arm, toe,* and *rib.*
23. C. sweets
24. color
25. Grandpa's apples have the best **taste** in the whole **state.**

Bonus Builder #5: Because there was **no table** in the operating room, the notable surgeon was **not able** to perform surgery.

Page 8
26. Change *report* to *resort*.
27. A *sleuth* is a detective. Students' sentences will vary. Possible sentence: The sleuth is trying to find clues to help solve the mysterious theft.
28. spring, summer, fall
29. Students' answers will vary. Possible answers are *clever, creative, bright, intelligent, smart,* and *inventive.*
30. Don't count your chickens before they're hatched.

Bonus Builder #6: Students' answers will vary. *Pnifs* and *pnufs* can be any pet, such as a dog, cat, hamster, etc. *Valooms* can be any wild pet, such as a skunk.

Page 9
31. shoebo**x,** colored mar**kers,** red and blue con**struction p**aper, yarn or strin**g,** senten**ce st**rips
32. flour
33. Students' answers will vary. Possible endings should rhyme with *kid.*
34. Students' answers may vary. Possible answers include working on a scrapbook or project.
35. Two heads are better than one.

Bonus Builder #7: Samantha frowned. She didn't agree with Duncan's **decision.** She wanted to **eat** before they left for the stadium. It was **5 P.M.** now, and it'd be **7 P.M.** before they arrived. **So** Samantha packed a **snack.**

Page 10
36. rapid–slow
37. blend
38. relish
39. Students' synonyms will vary. Possible answers include *firm, solid, strong, rigid* and *difficult, harsh, perplexing,* etc.
40. Students' solutions will vary. One possible solution is *east, past, pest, west.*

Bonus Builder #8:

P	E	S	T
E	C	H	O
S	H	O	W
T	O	W	N

Answer Keys

Page 11
41. speck, fleck
42. catsup, noon
43. a—assemble, b—build, c—construct or create
44. cut–carve, fat–plump
45. asleep–awake

Bonus Builder #9: A. heavy light, B. few lots, C. bottom top

Page 12
46. locks
47. complex, simple
48. A. upset or upturn, B. understand, C. useless, unable, or unsuccessful
49. smooth, rough
50. A. grab, B. gab, C. drab

Bonus Builder #10: A. eats, B. see, C. part, D. last, E. tutor

Page 13
51. Students' answers may vary. One possible solution is *sick, silk, sill, sell, well.*
52. stiff
53. bind, fasten, knot
54. inhabit, forgive
55. teach, coach

Bonus Builder #11: Students' answers may vary. One possible pair is *lose–gain.*

Page 14
56. scare–fright, rip–tear
57. Students' sentences will vary. Possible sentence: When the order of stock did not arrive on time, the store owner found herself in a tight spot.
58. sullen, glum
59. wrap, warp
60. later

Bonus Builder #12:

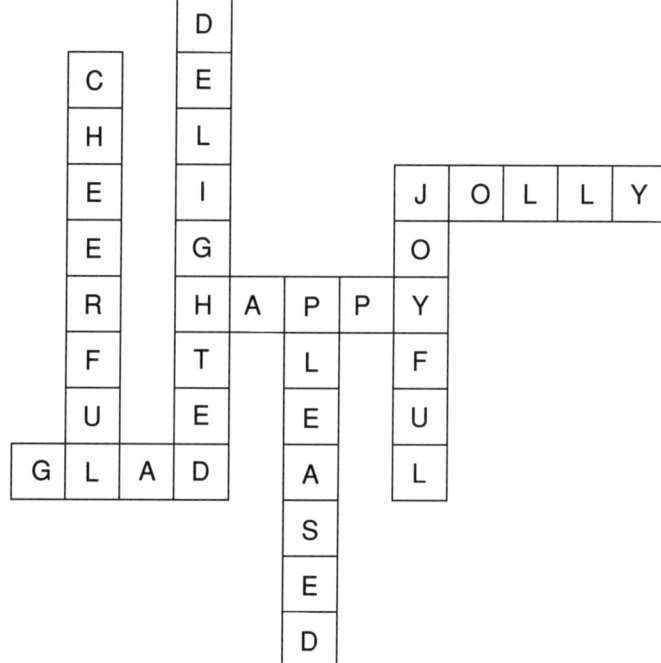

Page 15
61. occurrence
62. silent–noisy
63. figure
64. winsome, blackout
65. Students' answers will vary. One possible solution is *give, gave, rave, rake, take.*

Bonus Builder #13: The two words are *obligation* and *commitment.*

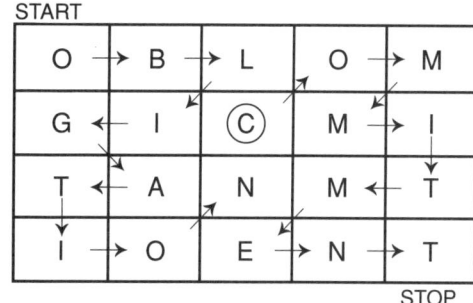

Page 16
66. light–dark
67. leave
68. bestow, donate, present
69. gigantic–miniature
70. A. stack, B. whack or smack, C. track, D. yak

Bonus Box #14: The synonym pairs are *peak–crest* and *resolve–settle.* The antonym pairs are *oppose–support* and *soar–descend.*

Page 17
71. I **do not know** which shirt **to choose**: the **red one** or the **blue** one.
72. A. toad–towed, B. carrot–carat
73. Students' answers will vary. Possible answers include *pare–pear, ware–wear, great–grate, stake–steak, tare–tear,* and *bear–bare.*
74. ceiling, sealing
75. The musical instruments are *cymbal* and *lyre. Cent* is a unit of money.

Bonus Builder #15: Students' answers will vary. Possible answers:

A—ant–aunt   M—main–mane
B—be–bee   N—not–knot
C—cents–sense   O—one–won
D—due–do   P—piece–peace
E—eight–ate   R—rain–rein
F—flew–flu   S—sum–some
G—gnu–new   T—through–threw
H—high–hi   U—urn–earn
I—isle–aisle   V—vale–veil
J—jam–jamb   W—whole–hole
K—know–no   Y—you–ewe
L—lessen–lesson

Page 18
76. Wit**h ear**ly care, **he re**ally should not need surgery. (hear–here)
77. allowed, beets
78. one–won, two–to–too, four–for–fore, eight–ate
79. Students' answers may vary. One possible answer is *groan, rang, ran, an, a* and *o, on, won, worn, grown.*
80. beau–bow

Bonus Builder #16: Students' answers will vary. Possible answers include *bare–bear, fair–fare, pair–pare–pear, there–their–they're, tare–tear, stare–stair,* and *ware–wear.*

Answer Keys

Page 19

81. Students' sentences will vary. Possible sentence: Mark used a pail of soapy water to wash the graffiti from the pale wall.
82. Students' answers will vary. Possible answers include *air–heir, no–know, gnu–new, cent–sent, write–right, wrap–rap, ring–wring, cell–sell,* and *one–won.*
83. **There** was a brief **pause** before she **made** the decision to **hire** a **new** mechanic to fix her car's **brakes.**
84. A. chord–cord, B. fir–fur
85. whole, hole

Bonus Builder #17: Students' sentences will vary. Possible sentence: She **sent** away **to** a company for **two** candles with a rose **scent** to give as gifts, but by the time the delivery man **rapped** on her door with the package, there wasn't time for them to be **wrapped.**

Page 20

86. *Pare* the *pear!*
87. Tools: *ax* and *awl.* To write a letter: *stationery.*
88. Students' answers will vary. Possible answers are *ax–acts, tax–tacks,* and *lax–lacks.*
89. Students' sentences will vary. Possible sentence: Tyler experienced a great amount of pain when he touched the hot grate.
90. mist, missed

Bonus Builder #18: Every word except *bide* and *picture* has a homophone: *rote–wrote, away–aweigh, ball–bawl, wring–ring, creak–creek, sow–so* (or *sow–sew*).

Page 21

91. principal, capital
92. Students' sentences will vary. Possible sentence: One has **seen** a **mist,** and the other has **missed** a **scene!**
93. He **guessed** that Paul's party **would be** a **great one.**
94. Students' answers may vary. Possible answers include *be–bee, sea–see, oh–owe,* and *tee–tea.*
95. waste, waist

Bonus Builder #19: Students' answers will vary. Possible answers include *by–buy–bye, do–dew–due, for–four–fore, so–sew–sow, pair–pare–pear, to–too–two, right–rite–write, you–ewe–yew,* and *rain–rein–reign.*

Page 22

96. Nick will travel to S**pain** soon, and he hopes to go to Ja**pan e**ventually. (pain–pane)
97. nose–knows
98. peek, peak
99. Students' answers will vary. Possible riddle: Why did Tommy have a tummy ache? Because he ate eight pizzas!
100. Students' answers will vary. Possible answers include *Maine–main–mane, Mary–merry–marry, Eve–eave, Forrest–forest, Beau–bow,* and *Rome–roam.*

Bonus Builder #20: Students' answers may vary. Possible solutions include *waist, wits, sit, is, I* and *a, at, ate, eats, waste.*

Page 23

101. people: assistants, attendants, beau, belle, boarder, knight, marshal, friar, nun, patients, prophet, serf; things to buy: bow, bell, border (for wallpaper), fryer
102. A. currant–current, B. colonel–kernel
103. Students' answers will vary. Possible answers include *chili–chilly, beat–beet, berry–bury, bread–bred, carat–carrot, cereal–serial, dough–doe, flour–flower, maize–maze, meat–meet, pear–pair,* and *stake–steak.*
104. Students' sentences will vary. Possible sentence: Mrs. Bates used scissors to shear the sheer fabric into strips.
105. Students' sentences will vary. Possible sentence: "Who's going to help serve?" asked the teacher whose class won the pizza party.

Bonus Box #21: I'll–aisle–isle, I–aye–eye, you–ewe–yew, he'll–heal–heel, we'll–weal–wheel

Page 24

106. Students' answers will vary. Possible answers include *run, swim, sit, hit, knit, jab, grab, hop,* and *chop.*
107. A. superintendent, B. resident, C. recipient
108. in-, ex-
109. A. biographer, writer, or author; B. manicurist; C. astronomer
110. hexagonal: 6, octagonal: 8, triangular: 3

Bonus Builder #22: Students' answers may vary. Possible words include *retest, retested, retesting, repack, repacked, repacking, unpack, unpacked, unpacking, mismatch, mismatched, mismatching,* and *rematch.*

Page 25

111. co-
112. useful, -less
113. Students' answers will vary. Possible answers include *walk, drink, eat, sew, cook, build, work, catch, throw,* and *climb.*
114. Students' answers will vary. One possible answer is *sink.* Adding the prefix *un-* and the suffix *-able* makes the word *unsinkable.* Possible sentence: Many people thought the *Titanic* was unsinkable.
115. A. immovable or immobile, B. illegal, C. underfed or malnourished

Bonus Builder #23: A. specialist, B. landlocked, C. punishment

Page 26

116. *gram* to form *program, pound* to form *propound,* and *ton* to form *proton*
117. Students' answers will vary. Possible answers include *un-, ir-, im-, in-,* and *il-.*
118. hoping, flying
119. happier
120. misbehave, misconduct, misfortune

Bonus Builder #24: Students' answers will vary. Possible answers include *mist, male, able, table, stab, stable, take, tale, sale, sake,* and *stake.*

Answer Keys

Page 27
121. fly, fry, try, buy, cry, pry
122. Students' answers will vary. One possible answer is *think*. Adding the prefix *un-* and the suffix *-able* to *think* makes the word *unthinkable*. Possible sentence: After Allison's accident, the idea of her taking a second job was unthinkable.
123. bookkeeper
124. Students' answers will vary. Possible answers are *five (fifth), nine (ninth), twelve (twelfth), and twenty (twentieth)*.
125. Students' answers will vary. One possible answer is *shut, nod, hat*.

Bonus Builder #25: Students' answers will vary. Possible answers include *able, band, content, grace, obedient, advantage, believe, continue, honest, order, agree, charge, cover, infect, own, appear, comfort, favor, like, regard, appoint, connect, loyal,* and *satisfy*.

Page 28
126. Each bicycle has two wheels. Each tricycle has three wheels. The unicycle has one wheel. So (4 x 2 wheels) + (3 x 3 wheels) + 1 wheel = 18 wheels.
127. forgetful
128. doubtful
129. *under-*
130. indecisive or undecided

Bonus Builder #26: A. needless, B. steering, C. excelled

Page 29
131. A. editor, B. seamstress, C. cartoonist
132. *-ion*
133. A. irreversible, B. undeniable, C. oversized
134. two sets: *un-, re-*
135. Students' answers will vary. One possible answer is *unruffled* (un + ruffle + ed).

Bonus Builder #27: Students' answers will vary. Possible answers are *unthinking, unquenchable, dishonored, unlisted, unfairly, fairness, prying,* and *endangerment*.

Page 30
136. A. international, B. autobiography, C. hemisphere
137. Students' answers will vary. Possible answers are *macrocosm—universe, megacycle—one million cycles,* and *microscale—a very small scale*.
138. talk—talkative, earth—earthen, bake—baked, danger—dangerous, sun—sunny, joy—joyous, metal—metallic
139. Students' answers will vary. Possible answers are *annoyance, resistance, vacancy, fascination, accuracy, freedom, absence, frequency, bravery, grandeur, childhood, necessity, civilization, amusement, friendship, tension, length, attention, gratitude,* and *loyalty*.
140. narrate—narration, compute—computation, visit—visitation, sum—summation, declare—declaration, recite—recitation, vocalize—vocalization. The word *visit* did not need a change in spelling.

Bonus Box #28: Students' answers will vary. Possible answers are *afternoon, afterward, antebellum, epilogue, epitaph, postpone, postscript, preamble, prefix,* and *prologue*.

Page 31
141. omnibus
142. Melba toast is a thin, crisp toast named after singer Nellie Melba. The dessert peach melba also bears her name.
143. sole
144. **ra**dio **d**etecting **a**nd **r**anging
145. Students' answers will vary. Possible answers are *manicure*—care of the hands, *manual*—something operated with the hands, *manuscript*—something written or typed by hand, and *manufacture*—to make by hand.

Bonus Builder #29: bouquet, crochet

Page 32
146. A. ballet, B. chalet
147. Students' answers will vary. Possible answers are *audio, audition, audible, audience,* and *auditorium*.
148. smoke and fog
149. the Charleston (Charleston, South Carolina)
150. Bloomers are full trousers gathered at the ankle. They were named after Amelia Bloomer, a woman who lived in the 1800s and campaigned for women's voting rights.

Bonus Builder #30: Students' answers will vary. Possible answers: Don't cry over milled spilk. Dill waters run steep.

Page 33
151. **M**obile **A**rmy **S**urgical **H**ospital
152. *Optical* is from the Greek word *optikos,* which means "eye."
153. *Flu* is the shortened form of *influenza*.
154. bureau
155. tangerine

Bonus Builder #31: A. Alexander G. Bell, B. Daniel Salmon, C. Louis Pasteur, D. Alessandro Volta, E. James Watt

Page 34
156. Students' answers will vary. Possible answers are *microscope, telescope,* and *periscope*.
157. a sideburn
158. breakfast, lunch
159. bon voyage
160. dos

Bonus Builder #32: A. **z**one **i**mprovement **p**lan, B. **U**nited **N**ations **I**nternational **C**hildren's **E**mergency **F**und, C. **R**eserve **O**fficer's **T**raining **C**orps, D. **Sun** **O**il **Co**mpany, E. **N**ational **A**ssociation for **S**tock **C**ar **A**uto **R**acing

Answer Keys

Page 35
161. chauffeur
162. **p**ersonal **i**dentification **n**umber
163. foreigner
164. Students' answers will vary. Possible answers are *gardenia* (Alexander Garden), *begonia* (Michel Begon), *magnolia* (Pierre Magnol), *dahlia* (Anders Dahl), and *poinsettia* (Joel R. Poinsett).
165. fiesta, siesta

Bonus Builder #33: Students' answers will vary.

Page 36
166. kindergarten
167. Theodore "Teddy" Roosevelt
168. solution
169. Students' answers will vary. Possible answers are *signature, signal, significant,* and *insignia.*
170. conclude

Bonus Builder #34: A. fear of cats, B. fear of heights or high places, C. fear of small places, D. fear of people, E. fear of birds

Page 37
171. Students' sentences with *etc.* will vary.
172. A. Janus—January, B. Mars—March, C. Maia—May
173. *BLT* stands for **b**acon, **l**ettuce, and **t**omato. *ASAP* stands for **as s**oon **as p**ossible.
174. A. television, marathon; B. picture, element; C. travel, monologue; D. motor, cross country; E. splash, spatter
175. A. typo—typographical error, B. vet—veteran (or veterinarian), C. limo—limousine, D. fridge—refrigerator. Students' sentences will vary.

Bonus Builder #35: Students' answers will vary.

Page 38
176. A. We're in **hot** water now! B. You're pulling my **leg!** C. Let's just **bury** the hatchet.
177. Reading between the lines. It means to understand more than is directly stated.
178. Students' answers will vary. Possible answer: Her words were scissors, cutting apart all hopes for peace and restoration.
179. A. face, B. shoulder, C. head
180. hyperbole

Bonus Builder #36: Students' answers will vary.

Page 39
181. The missing word is *pull*. A. to do one's share of the work, B. to carry out a task in spite of difficulties, C. to use some hidden influence or control
182. A simile compares two unlike things using *like* or *as*. A metaphor compares two unlike things directly without using *like* or *as*.
183. Students' answers will vary. Possible answers: eat your heart out, eat your words, have your cake and eat it too, and eat like a bird.
184. Students' answers will vary. Possible answers: A. ate like my dad when he's missed both his breakfast and lunch, B. walked like someone on snowshoes for the first time, C. shone like the star on our Christmas tree
185. as happy as a lark

Bonus Builder #37: Students' answers will vary. Possible answers: He has something up his sleeve. (He is behaving in a secretive manner.); She's living on a shoestring. (She's living on a small amount of money.); I wouldn't want to be in his shoes. (I wouldn't want to be in his position.)

Page 40
186. Students' answers will vary.
187. Students' answers will vary. Possible answer: My pet fish smiled at me as I fed him.
188. broken heart
189. Students' answers will vary. Possible answers: A. green with envy, a green thumb; B. blue-chip stock, it happens once in a blue moon; C. red-carpet treatment, painting the town red
190. Students' answers will vary. Possible answers are hot under the collar, fit to be tied, seeing red, having the blues, and blowing his stack. Students' sentences will vary.

Bonus Builder #38: I have a bone to pick with you!

Page 41
191. A. crow, B. pig, C. dogs
192. Students' sentences will vary.
193. If this rain keeps up, it won't come down!
194. Students' answers will vary.
195. Students' answers will vary.

Bonus Builder #39: Students' answers will vary.

Page 42
196. Students' answers will vary.
197. A. silver (Something good can be found in every difficult situation.), B. gold (He is kind and generous.), C. blue (It came without warning.)
198. safety in numbers
199. break
200. Students' answers will vary. Possible answers include throw in the towel, throw one's weight around, throw a party, and throw light on.

Bonus Builder #40: Students' answers will vary. Possible answers are a *keynote address* (a speech containing information of primary interest to a gathering of people), *jump on the bandwagon* (to join a popular group or cause), and *fiddle around* (to tinker harmlessly or tamper destructively with something).

Page 43
201. Students' answers will vary.
202. Students' sentences will vary.
203. A. ear, B. eye, C. hair or face
204. Take the cake. It means to carry off the prize or to rank first. Students' sentences will vary. Possible sentence: This year, all the science fair projects are excellent, but Keith's really takes the cake.
205. Students' answers will vary.

Bonus Builder #41: Students' answers and sentences will vary. Possible similes are as strong as an ox, as busy as a bee, as happy as a lark, as hungry as a bear, as sly as a fox, as quiet as a mouse, as stubborn as a mule, as meek as a lamb, laughed like a hyena, drank like a fish, walked like an elephant, waddled like a duck, and worked like a horse.